# HAWKER

# Books by Robert Peters

## Poetry

FOURTEEN POEMS
SONGS FOR A SON
THE SOW'S HEAD AND OTHER POEMS
EIGHTEEN POEMS
BYRON EXHUMED
RED MIDNIGHT MOON
CONNECTIONS: In the English Lake District
HOLY COW: Parable Poems
COOL ZEBRAS OF LIGHT
BRONCHIAL TANGLE, HEART SYSTEM
THE GIFT TO BE SIMPLE: A Garland for Ann Lee Founder of the Shakers
THE POET AS ICE-SKATER
GAUGUIN'S CHAIR: Selected Poems
HAWTHORNE
THE DROWNED MAN TO THE FISH
CELEBRITIES: In Memory of Margaret Dumont
THE PICNIC IN THE SNOW: Ludwig II of Bavaria
LUDWIG: The Acting Version
WHAT DILLINGER MEANT TO ME

## Criticism

THE CROWNS OF APOLLO: Swinburne's Principles of Literature and Art
PIONEERS OF MODERN POETRY (with George Hitchcock)
THE GREAT AMERICAN POETRY BAKE-OFF: First and Second Series
THE PETERS BLACK AND BLUE GUIDE TO CURRENT LITERARY
    PERIODICALS

# Robert Peters

# HAWKER

1984

Greensboro: Unicorn Press, Inc.

. Some of these poems have appeared previously in the following periodicals and are reprinted with the kind permission of their editors:

ABRAXAS, ANGEL'S FLIGHT, BELOIT POETRY JOURNAL, BERKELEY POETRY REVIEW, NEW LETTERS, POET-LORE, POETRY SOCIETY OF AMERICA BULLETIN (1982), THE REAPER, and THE SALTHOUSE MISCELLANY.

The author received the Poetry Society of America's Alice Faye di Castagnola Prize for HAWKER in 1982

Typeset in 14/14 *Deepdene* by Anita Richardson, printed by Inter-Collegiate-Press on 70# "Neutral Natural," an acid-free sheet, and hand-bound at Unicorn Press. Designed by Alan Brilliant. All *rights reserved*.

**Library of Congress Cataloguing-in-Progress Data:**

ISBN 0-87775-165-X, *cloth*
ISBN 0-87775-166-8, *paper*
ISBN 0-87775-164-1, *signed*

UNICORN PRESS, INC.
P.O. Box 3307
Greensboro, NC 27402

FOR *Janine Dakyns* and *Paul Trachtenberg,* with much affection. And with special thanks to *Grace Schulman, Carolyn Forché,* and *Jerome Mazzarro,* judges for the Poetry Society of America who awarded an earlier version of this manuscript the Alice Faye di Castagnola Prize, in 1982.

# LIST OF POEMS

Hawker to Peters in a Dream /2

## PART ONE: BUCOLICS

The Land /7
"How over-fond" /8
Hummingbirds, Bees, and Fritillaries /9
Elves on a Snowy Branch /10
Orchard Fecundity /11
A Flower /12
Rosy Beauties Laid to Rest /13
Hostel, with Clerics /14
Tamar River Cornish Pie /15
Animals, Oh! /16
Cows /17
My Old Ewe /18
Gyp, My Loving Big Black Pig /19
The Diseases of Swine /20
On Moving Rooks from My Chimney /21

## PART TWO: HAWKER'S CHURCH: HIS LOVE, HIS JOY

Churchyard Quadrants /25
An Ancient Priest Buried in Morwenstowe /26
Pious Ladies /27
Harvest Ritual /28
The Glories of My Church /29
Methodists /32
Cleaning out the Church /33
A Riddle From the Pulpit /34
St. Mark's School /35
A Spirit Mathematics for Tables and Oranges /36
This Wretched Parish /38
Needy Family /40
Consumption /42

Prawns /43
Plum-Pudding /44


PART THREE: HOLY SAINT MORWENNA

Song /47
Celtic Morwenna, Daughter of King Breachan /48
The Vivid Bird /50
Trees and Flowers /52
Merry-Maidens /53


PART FOUR: POOR DROWNED SAILORS

On Cornish Wreckers /61
Two Former Wreckers /62
Smuggler Horses /63
Off Bude, Cornwall /65
On Trying to Reach A Ship in Distress /66
The Wreck of the Caledonia /68


PART FIVE: WITCHES, WARLOCKS, AND CHARACTERS

"Beating rain, howling wind" /73
Bewitched Animals /74
Webby Pryce /75
Black John /76
Tony Cleverdon /78
Christiana Manning /79
First Storm in Paradise /80
How to Gain the Evil Eye /81
All is the Idea, the Idea is All /82
Pastoral Advice /84
Memento Mori Ragout /85

PART SIX: OPIUM

On Toothaches and Opium /89
Opium /92
Turks and Englishmen /93
Fistulas /94
Opium Pipe /95
False Teeth /96
The Tentacula of Cancer /97
"My mouth is packed with ocean sand" /98
Flame Tongues /99
"Porphyry, opal, emerald, and chrysolite" /100
Prison Hallucination /101
Opium Haze Christmas Poem /103
Opium Song /105
A Last Word /107

*A brief introduction by the author appears before the poems and a brief biography of the author after the poems.*

## ROBERT STEPHEN HAWKER: *Vicar of Morwenstowe*

This work is based on the life of the eccentric Cornish vicar, Robert Stephen Hawker (1802-1875), whose church, home, and parish I visited in 1981, guided there by Janine Dakyns and accompanied by my friend, fellow-poet Paul Trachtenberg. Morwenstowe, bleak and isolated, is less than a mile from the 400' cliffs overlooking a wild portion of the Cornish coast noted for shipwrecks—the Torrey Canyon foundered there. In the cliff above the horrendous bay, Hawker imbedded a hut he built of wood salvaged from wrecks. Here he would sit for hours waiting for drowned sailors, composing poems, and entertaining angels and Saint Morwenna, the legendary Celtic visionary. Hawker was obsessed with rescuing dead sailors washed ashore. He buried over 150 bodies in his churchyard.

He dressed eccentrically, in claret cassock, a yellow wool poncho, fisherman's boots and sweater, and a bright red hat. He always wore a purple patch visible on his costume, to mark the spot where the spear struck Christ. He liked animals to attend his church services, and was followed everywhere by a pet Berkshire pig Gyp. He had an addiction for playing mermaid. As a boy he was known as "the Merry maid of Plymouth." As vicar, he enjoyed regaling his unwitting flock by posing in the bay, draped in seaweed, flashing a mirror in the moonlight and singing. The parishioners never knew his secret. In later years, after the death of his wife Charlotte (she was 80, and twice his age), he turned to opium to relieve his distress, thereby intensifying his visions and his paranoia. Over sixty, he married a young Belgian girl, fathered three daughters, and converted to his wife's religion, Roman Catholicism. He died at age 75.

Not only was Hawker a notable poet and essayist (he wrote the Cornish National Anthem and books of essays and various miscellanies), but he was a great individual, a virtue suspect in our time. He is of the tradition of nineteenth century individualists that includes Thomas Carlyle, John Stuart Mill, George Eliot, Henry Thoreau, Walt Whitman, and Ralph Waldo Emerson. Hawker is one of the most complex humans I have ever encountered. For details I have found these books useful: Piers Brendon, *Hawker of Morwenstowe* (London, 1975); S. Baring-Gould, *The Vicar of Morwenstowe* (London, 1949); Hawker's poems and prose; and Nathaniel Hawthorne's more obscure writings.

# HAWKER

A man is under the crassest necessity
to break down the pinnacles of his moods.

—William Carlos Williams, *Paterson*

# HAWKER TO PETERS IN A DREAM

Write, Hawker said,
that I am lying on my side,
in a meadow,
during a cold rain, weeping.
I am wearing my yellow poncho
over my purple cassock
and my leather gaiters.
My hat was last seen, with wings,
wafting over the bay,
near the reefs
where so many ships have crashed
where I have just found such sad morsels
of more poor dear sailors:
4 haunches without femurs. 6 lorn feet.
5 ribcages sea-weed strewn. 3 bearded
faces without ears (scraped off by rocks),
and 1 lone penis with a crayfish
affixed thereto.

After washing the carnage
in sandalwood crushed in oil,
I blessed each piece,
bestowing names—
as an angel inscribed them
on my mind, during prayers.
I kissed the rigid lips
of the last face I buried.
The teeth struck mine
and exuded a noisome odor
which I did not much like.

Write, Hawker said,
that I shall lie here 'til morning
when the skies shimmer, rooks stir hither,
and sheep once again leave their cotes.
Then I shall rise, and Mrs. Hawker
though she is in much pain, and aging,
will hobble out to meet me with cheer
and fresh tea.  I do this work
in the only way I know, in faith
that these wretched bits so foully rent,
soaked, and decomposed, will be
restored to light. God's ragged puzzle
a whole again.  I am his Vicar.

# PART ONE:
## BUCOLICS

# THE LAND

My seaward boundary
is a bold and rocky shore,
an interchange of headland
and a 450' gorge.
The valleys gush with torrents.

My mere parish,
my remote glebe,
has severed me
from well-nigh
the merry hum of men.
Mine is a bounded orb.

Cacodemons leap out
and agathodemons
supplant them.

Here the falcon soars.
And choughs, if you
are attentive, chatter
*King Arthur, King Arthur.*
O blessed land!

How over-fond the earth seems of its air
this morning!

# HUMMINGBIRDS, BEES, AND FRITILLARIES

## 1

Little spiritual visitants
deign to sip airy food
from my nectar cups.
Hummingbirds in my bean blossoms.

## 2

A rare fritillary
shimmers near a willow
flaunting
in the chilly breeze
his dark red velvet cloak
with golden borders.

## 3

Bees bury their furry bodies
in my squash-flowers
and emerge painted with dust.
They give back nothing in requital
of what my garden contributes.
Yet, my life is far sweeter for their honey.

# ELVES ON A SNOWY BRANCH

An oak-tree branch, snow-crammed
with a dozen merry elves in a row
in German leather pants
with buttons as large as ox-eyes.
Tasselled multi-colored caps.

I mean to lead them
through a carol.
But they toss elf-dust in my eyes,
and chatter.
I had not counted sufficiently
on the behavior of elves in these parts.

## ORCHARD FECUNDITY

An apple thumps in the grass
thumps with a breeze attendant,
impelled to tumble from a perfect ripeness.

My pear trees fling down bushels.
The peaches torment me.
There's more than I can eat,
or without perplexity give to the needy.
The hedges are livid with whortleberries.

I'll pile a cache below the altar.

# A FLOWER

## 1

I am too rough. . .language
without grace, syllables without style.
May I begin again?
Thank you.

Women dismember men
who dismember trees—
rituals of terrible comfort
marriages smeared with nard
thick mustard-colored loins
and lacquered posteriors.

## 2

Despite her pox,
I risk my life for her
by hanging perpendicular
to the boiling sea
gathering flowers
from their crannies.

She's a milkmaid
She lips thick cream
from which white bats flit,
bats of incredible beauty.
Below its flow
the sea waits for her.

# ROSY BEAUTIES LAID TO REST

Grass strewn
with pine shavings
and chips of chestnut joists.

The germ of a castor bean
shoots up.  Amid the unfolding
leaves, a perfect flower.

Momentary footsteps
on lightbeams,
airy figures,
bloodless.

A bluebell clappers
for Oberon to pluck
its tongue.

The rosiest beauty is at last
a pale ghost,
mouldering hair, a few bones.

# HOSTEL, WITH CLERICS

The village reeked
of onions, cheese, and swine.
Each cubic inch of air
was stale
as the bell tolled nine.

Joan Treworgy
flubby and interjectional
received us at her inn:
a hot room with hard beds
and a solitary casement stuck shut
flanked by a glazed cupboard.

At the dawn's first splutter
we crossed the bridge
to view the mast and rigging
of a ship.
Above us lay the mists,
the breaths
of the village snorers.

The road
was a Jacob's ladder
out of this fen-hole.

# TAMAR RIVER CORNISH PIE

Dorothy Dinglett's oven entrance
is a vast church door:
rye loaves, barley buns,
and oat cakes sugared
fatten her board.
A hillock of brown dough
a reeking small volcano
with vented puffs of savory vapor.

When the dish is broken open
we are astounded at the tumble
of oysters, conger-eels, and pilchards
mixed piece-meal
in clotted cream and butter.

Old Satan, they say,
never crossed the Tamar
for fear he would be cast
beneath a savory Cornish crust.

# ANIMALS, OH!

Nine cats have I this season, in church and out.
They follow me about, regaling the air
with their mews, rubbing my legs
with their whiskers.

Let them lap warm milk in the belfry
and squat in the vestry.

Old Cat though has sorely vexed me. He ate a mouse
in Church on Sunday, near the altar.
I excommunicate him. He leaves me grieving.
Animals are the visible attributes of God
roaming this earth.

# COWS

Among the gentlest
of breathing creatures
is the cow.

None shows more
passionate tenderness
for its young
when deprived of them.

None shows more wonderfully
striated colors in its eyes
when it's busy at its cud.

None steps more gracefully,
even full-uddered,
through a slimy pond,
barely nicking the lilies.

And when it's beaten
it hunches its long
backbone and shudders
and bunches together
with other cows for protection.

I love these wholesome creatures.

# MY OLD EWE

The curly ewe
lies atop a hill of grass,
on her side, where she died.
Her tongue depends.  A stream of ants,
such as I have never seen,
scurry through her mouth.
Another horrendous mass
has eaten a path
through her cornea, ingress
to the vitreous humor.
Soon her hide will float
from her bones towards America.

If she were a lioness
bees would swell, in a honeycomb,
amidst the putrefaction.
A sermon lurks hereabouts.
Dear ewe.  Dear eye.

# GYP, MY LOVING BIG BLACK PIG

An Acrostic Poem

Gyp goes with me everywhere:
You'll find him in church on a Sunday
Pillowed upon clean straw, to the east of the altar

Muffling his whiffles, reserving grunts of pleasure,
Yeasty eructations, for the noisier hymns and carols.

Lively and contented, wiggling his quirky tail
Over the coombes and valleys, he trots behind the
Vicar as he visits his parishioners —
In house, in cot, in glebe and pasture,
Never once despoiling a humble hearth-stone.
Glad to be sociable, he jiggles his globular testes.

Brushing a floppy ear means he wants a good scratching.
In storm, in sun, the elements ne'er dissuade him:
Gloriously he wallows in the finest muck-holes

Believing he's in Paradise, awash in tarry ichor.
Later I must scrub him and oil his hide with suet.
After that we'll take our tea with good Dorothy Dinglett.
Coarse he is outside 'tis true, but within he's all refinement.
Know, ye cynics, and be warned: and model your own deportment

Pig-wise, Gyp-wise. You'll surely feel an improvement
In manners as well as morals. And when you next devour pork
Grant a special whiff of thanks to Black Gyp and his tribe.

# THE DISEASES OF SWINE

Hog cholera (swine fever)
rages the world over.
Infected pork is hazardous.

Erysipelas causes lesions,
unthriftiness,
necrosis and arthritis.

Gastroenteritis attacks new piglets.
Haemorrhagic dysentery
is an infectious virus.

Brucellosis maims
the spinal cord and testes.
Treatment is ineffective.

Beware leptospirosis,
swine pox and influenza,
ictero-anemia and rhinitis.

Soap your swine,
nourish them well.
Their diseases
do kill humans.

# ON MOVING ROOKS FROM MY CHIMNEY

I'm exhausted. I've moved
a pair of rooks
from the west chimney.
I lodged the nest
in an oak.
The birds seem easy there,
croaking and obstreperously cawing.

Quiet swifts (bless them) reside now
in the flue.  They are no less
God's creatures, no less my friends.
The zig-zag in the stone
echoes patterns on their wings.

# PART TWO:
# HAWKER'S CHURCH:
# HIS LOVE, HIS JOY

# CHURCHYARD QUADRANTS

North Yard is devoid of graves.
There's the Devil's dominion.
East Yard is for oracles,
the special gate to the throne of God.
West is for the populace, a Galilee of nations.
South, the land of mid-day, is never sacred.

# AN ANCIENT PRIEST BURIED IN MORWENSTOWE WITH HIS FEET TO THE WEST

## 1

At the outshine of the Last Day,
as Archangels flay the air with trumpets,
like soldiers from their sleep,
the dead creep from the dust
and suddenly
stand erect before the Son of Man.

We bury our dead
with their heads to the west.

## 2

Apostles and priests
fly through the air
to meet Him in the East.

Apostles and priests
assist the Lord
with His judgments.

They officiate over men—
those battalions of rapscallions,
the saints and the damned.

## PIOUS LADIES

Pious ladies
cling to me like ivy to a wall.
They think to reach Heaven
by clutching my coat-tails.
I'll trounce them!
I'll wear a spencer!

# HARVEST RITUAL

### 1

Summer squash, I say
provide an array
of endless urns and vases,
shallow or deep,
plain or scalloped.
A sculptor would find them useful
for imitating.

### 2

Beneath the leaves,
crook-neck squash
turn their rotundities.

Cabbages swell.
Their hearts encumbered
burst asunder,
as if to please us
by performing well.

### 3

Smoking, these vegetable children
grace our tables.

# THE GLORIES OF MY CHURCH

Tell of the boss
remarkable in mid-roof,
of Solomon's pentacle,
that five-angled figure
engraved on emerald,
wherewith he ruled his demons.

Tell of the Norman doorway,
900 A.D., with its semicircular
arch-head
sustained by half-piers,
the capitals adorned
with zigzag devices,
the curve crowned
with chevron moldings.

Tell of the mermaid,
dolphin, and grampus
crowning the arch
guarded by dragons crouched
before a lamb.

Tell of the western window,
ill-proportioned, askew:
when Christ died
his head drooped tenderly
to his right shoulder.

Tell of the ancient piscina
located where I struck the chancel
and found it hollow.

Beneath was an arch
filled with a jumble of carved work
and a crushed drain.

Tell of the Norman font
girded by a molded cable fixed
to the apse, its uncouth lip
chiselled in times of rude taste
and facile symbolism,
its waters emergent from St. John's
sweet well beneath the stones.

Tell of the chancel roof,
carved by early Christians:
the Norman rose and the fleur-de-lis.
(The Rose of Sharon is our Lord,
the Lily of the Vale is His mother).
A double-necked eagle,
an old, odd image,
is the Holy Ghost.
Vine-roots sprout from the altar.
Stems travel over the screen
to the nave where tendrils cling
and luscious grape-clusters swing.

*Morwenstowe:*
One church to grasp,
and a single roof to bend over all.  Selah.

Still points the tower, and pleads the bell;
    The solemn arches breathe in stone;
Window and wall have lips to tell
    The mighty faith of days unknown.
Yea! flood, and breeze, and battle-shock
    Shall beat upon this church in vain:
She stands, a daughter of the rock,
    The changeless God's eternal fane.*

*The final stanza of Hawker's "Morwennae Statio."

# METHODISTS

John Wesley's Chapel girls
justify unchastity
by wallowing in
a heresy—
an angel informs them
in their majority
that no matter their leprosy
they have an angel-home eternally.
Hence, these lissome
followers of Wesley
parade their bastards
shamelessly.
Degraded is this English nation.

# CLEANING OUT THE CHURCH

A curate refurbishes my church
by casting out rubbish:
puce garlands, an old crêche,
decayed sandal-wood,
straw somewhat befouled
by animals attending services,
old funeral wreaths,
roses and daisies
from mid-summer festivities,
scraps of prayer-books, Bibles,
candle-ends, ceremonial lace,
de-fumed mouse-corpses as dry
as parchment, the carcass
of an old friendly one-eyed cat.

He thinks his effort
will assist his preferment.

I let him wriggle
then advise him with a smile
to complete the pile
by sitting on top of it!

"A meek and faithful heart be thine.
Mark well this dusty lumber.
Summer fruit takes steadfast root
in dank and resistant soils.
So wheel this rubbish back
and pile it near the chancel.
'Twill make a cozy slumber-spot
for dear old Gyp's black swine-soul."

# A RIDDLE FROM THE PULPIT

Which bank of the Tamar River
is the right and which the left?

Do circumstances of position
vary the possibilities?

I think not, friend, for
the position of the spectator

is fixed by custom:
you must always stand

with your back to the source,
with your eyes on the current.

Thus, the right bank lies *absolutely*
on your right, and not *relatively* only,

as would be the case for a vestibule,
if a river were not concerned.

We position our backs
toward Heaven, safe, and face
the purling of our lives.

Thus, the right is always on our right.
From thence we cast out prayers.

## ST MARK'S SCHOOL

I built this school
for teaching the Golden Rule.

Patrick O'Carroll
(he croaked like a frog)
complained of his salary,
£20 annually.
I dismissed
the malignant Fenian.

I hired Arthur Truss,
a slaver from Barbados
who brought his mulatto wife
to Morwenstowe.
I let him go.

John Littlejohn
one-armed and poor,
eked out his salary
as parish postmaster.
I catechize on Fridays.
We shall instruct
in Geography soon.

## 1

An unfair division occurs
when a child
who separates an orange
is allowed to choose
his own portion.

An angel decrees
this fair division:
either child may divide,
but *the other* shall have
the choice. The divider
inherits any disadvantage
from an inept division.

## 2

Tables may or may not be
geometries.
A square table has
polar extremities,
a head and a foot,
a perihelion and an aphelion,
and equatorial sides
all ranked and liveried.

The center of a round table shifts—
the King may seat himself
at any point around the rim.
Retainers and slaves behave
as orange-bits, in relation
to their King or Vicar.

Right-angled, triangular
tables are Lucifer's.
He subtends all tenants
of the hypotenuse.
He is much nobler than they,
an Atlas fairer than the globe
he carries.

<br>

3

<br>

As Vicar
I shift tables
as I would split oranges.
I pronounce this square table round,
this table on which I write.
I decree that curved table
in the vestibule to be square.
Let my flock puzzle over
my theorems, jiggling their spirits,
Selah!

Vivacious human properties
are not written up in theologies.
Books on religion are impertinent—
feathers, or else, lumps of lead.
Unlettered swains rest easily in their beds.
Ampersands and verbs skip not
through the pasturage of their tousled heads.

# THIS WRETCHED PARISH

This parish
is the blighted lost land
of Noah.
Workers receive eight
shillings a week, the least pay
in the shire.  A glass or two
of cider at harvest-time.
A worker eats but a slab of bread
per day.  He is delighted
if the farmer offer a saucer of milk.

Thirty years ago
when I came to Morwenstowe
each laborer had his pig
and his potato patch.  No more!
Cottages are hovels
unfit for cattle,
without good water, or
closet accommodation.
The sexes mingle
on promiscuous pallets.

The worst killer is scarlet fever
followed by
influenza, smallpox, and diphtheria.
Rheumatism is universal.
There is seldom a change
of clothes.  Wet garb soaks
the body of the possessor.

Old Martin Spear
recovered from cholera
(on the wax this year)
because, he said, he's been raised
on cheese. Today he'd have died—
for the poor eat starch.
There is no blood in potatoes.

Abigail Killian
drove her three children
to the forest for firewood.
They perished.

Jacob Verland, at wit's end,
haltered his wife, and drove her
to market, where he sold her
to the highest bidder.

Burning sandal-wood in church
is useless—as are prayers,
and gifts of food, faggots,
and coverlets for the poor.

I shall add more names
to the grisly list this year.

## NEEDY FAMILY

In a cottage at Wike St. Marie,
dwells a wretched family of three:
John Bonaventure, his wife
and daughter, all former Dissenters.
The roof thatch is mouldering.
The cobbed walls are falling.

Squire Gall is peeved
at Bonaventure's keeping
of his forest-lands at Deeping
and has discharged him.
In this cruel winter
there is no succor
for this dear family of my converts.

At 3 A.M., restless,
I rouse Will Pooly.
I load his arms with coverlets, barley,
and a flitch of bacon.
I carry peat and brandy
and we hurry to the cottage
in a grove of alders.

The good wife is like snow
adrift against a paling.
Though still alive I greatly fear
she will be dead by morning.

I say a prayer, then cross her lips,
and dribble in some brandy.
We rip off all the old damp quilts
and replace them with the fresh ones.

40

Bonaventure's breath is short.
Catarrh has overwhelmed him.
I drench his throat with alcohol
and help him to the fire.

"Now do not fear, my man," I say.
"Tomorrow you'll be better. The Lord
doth keep the rook's breast warm,
and he will give thee blessing."

I return home at 6 A.M.
in time to rehearse my sermon.
I'll censure squires who abuse the poor
placed by the Lord in their keeping.
Old Squire Gall shall be upset
and will resent my "meddling."
To him I'll shout: "The world is stretch't,
as surely stretch't is Heaven.
In each, each man is equal to,
as each man has, his duties."

41

# CONSUMPTION

Walk through a forest.
Note the blaze of white paint on certain trees
marked thus by the forester, as ripe for the axe.

The vernal section of our population,
youths and maidens, a multi-
tudinous crowd, are blazoned
for slaughter, a premature *florilegium*
of blighted flowers.

The parishioners cough and die,
and I don't know why.
I am myself afflicted with pulmonary
affections, and I labor, I fear, in danger
of this horrid phthisis.
Bits of bloody lung and phlegm
spew from my mouth and nostrils.
Yet, the Lord, I trust,
will keep His shepherd safe.

# PRAWNS

Tristam Pentire
accompanied me
to Marsland Mouth,
two miles north
of the vicarage,
where we snared
fifty prawns,
larger
than any
caught at Widemouth.

We should have caught more,
but our net tore.

# PLUM-PUDDING

### 1

At a child's funeral,
his grave by a massive tree . . .
as I am reciting versicles,
a robin amongst the boughs
spills an exquisite trill.
(This was last week.)
We sang the service together,
the bird and I.
At each of my sentences,
a still small sound arose—
like an infant's laugh,
a cry of gladness,
From the Angel was it,
or the Bird?

### 2

I am plagued of late
by an ulcerated throat.
The physician (I should have
consulted a veterinarian!)
applies leeches, a scalding
mustard plaster, and has me swallow
a caustic solution
which greatly impairs my voice.

Despite the horrendous blistering
I keep ministering
to the sick.
This Christmas we shall be free, I pray,
to relish the puddings
Mrs. Hawker
offers
to every parish family.

# PART THREE:
# HOLY SAINT MORWENNA

# SONG

Devil's Ring, Dozmere Pool,
Dragon-crest of a Viking.

Kilmarth Tor and the Rowter,
Hail the Mort d'Arthur.

Cartha Martha, Tamar Spring
Celtic barbarians

Hennacliff and Raven's Crag
King Ethelwolf and Edith.

Morwenstowe, and dear Morwenna
Patron saint of Cornwall.

# CELTIC MORWENNA,
## DAUGHTER OF KING BREACHAN

An Acrostic Poem

Crown me with lilac.
Envelop my well in columbine.
Lean and quaff spring-water.
Tankards of rich pewter.
Imbibe this ancient streaming,
Cups of my tears enraptured.

Morwenna loves you, Hawker. The
Oasts of Heaven emit fresh manna.
Rest sweetly in my visions.
Westerly zephyrs waft me thither.
Easterly breezes bring oblivion.
Ne'er shall I quit thee.
Ne'er shall thy blood chill.
Ask of my largesse, as you will.

Deep is my well, as are my willowy shadows.
After great suffering, surcease follows.
Under my dingle a snow-drop's
Growing. Pluck it, protect it.
Healing is spiritual.
Taste angel-ichor, Heaven's sugary palate.
Eat and be whole: sciatica and neuralgia,
Rheums of diaphragm and sphincter, all shall ease.

Oreads and angels whirl round my holy fountain,
Flick drops upon the altar, sprinkle the chancel.

Kneel, dear Hawker, as I appear to you singing
In showered light.
Now stroke my vibrant tresses and
Groan out thy sorrows.  Award me thy

Body for purging and blessing.
Ranunculas of pity, anemones of misery!
Each sinner has his rung in the Holy
Ascension, on the path to Freedom.
Corrupt we rise, pure and eternal,
Hebrew and Gentile, entering Jerusalem:
Artichokes of bliss, ortolans and angels.
Nascent restoration of the wrenched and crippled.

# THE VIVID BIRD

## 1

Even if, Morwenna,
you were buried in
Constantinople
and not in Cornwall
I would still lave my body
in your stream,
as I do
to honor you
each spring.

## 2

Often I tell petitioners
I am with Thee
and can't be interrupted.

I mean to tell the truth.

You do approve.
You tell me so.

As an ailing man
I must protect myself,
however I can.

## 3

We morbid souls, Morwenna,
are preternaturally awake.
Hobgoblins clap shut and die.

This world
should recline
its hoary head
on a convenient pillow
for a long nap.

We awake
as dewy infants, shoving
our little coverlets aside
rimmed with hoar-frost.
We shout with glee
at the glorious morn
in the spring-kissed trees.

## 4

Come, crimson bird,
shift your wings,
tread air.
You've flown from Samarcand,
traversing Wales, in a gale.
Saint Morwenna said you'd arrive,
with talons knived.
Don't chop my eyes.
I'll need them
for entering Paradise.

# TREES AND FLOWERS

A moss-grown lilac
has cradled these
western windows
for forty years.
It pushes out leaves.
Lilacs follow
anemically.
Trees of paradise
should die
before they are decrepit.

Persons who are graceful
or chiefly ornamental
should also die
before they are wrinkled,
with mossy bark
and blighted foliage.

I am old,
with knobby cheeks and
contorted, freckled limbs.
I flaunt few blossoms,
few spiritual apples
for a straggler's needs.

# MERRY-MAIDENS

### 1

As I am walking to my hut
engaged in visionary chat
with Morwenna, saint
of mermaids, Old Richard
Bungly—suddenly,
before I can stop him,
hikes up his green jerkin
clears his nose and squeaks:

"How they do ride about
upon these waters
with such ruxles as there be
upon this mighty coast
is more than I can see.
Reverend Sir,
how do they (merry-maidens)
secure their looking-glasses
when the seas are all a-stir?"

"They are fastened, Richard,
to the creature's person,
as fins are to a fish.
Or by silver wires hooked
beneath and round a scale
where there'd be a navel
if merry-maids were gestational,
which they are not, being oviporal,
their babes born from mer-eggs
laid on the sea-floor,
fertilized by milt
expressed from the groins
of drowned sailors."

## 2

As a lad I rode
life's anchor at Plymouth.
On halcyon days I swam in the bay.

There I would swim and play
as naked as a jay,
bedecked with kelp.
I'd yelp like a walrus
and face the shore.

Then I would sing, and more! and more!
Ballads, chanteys, and limericks by the score.

The crowd would shout
'til toughs sailed out
with tainted fish débris.
Lisping, they flaunted
their genitals.
I was "the Merry-maid of Plymouth."

# 3

(Verses penned by Hawker, aged 15)

O sailor, dear, I chant to thee
From my rocky ledge out in the sea.

My siren tones of love and passion
Will lure you hither, and, in my fashion

I shall love you with my lips
And with my fishy hips.

When I embrace you in my arms so milky,
I'll ensnare you in my golden hair so kelpy:

> Together we shall plunge and dive
> To my grotto 'neath the sea,
> Where love shall we
> Perpetually.

# 4

## (May, 1859)

In full moonshine
I'd scurry down the steeps
and hurry through the deeps
to a granite boulder
where I'd plait seaweed
around my shoulders,
encase my lower limbs
in an oilskin
and sing, flashing moonbeams
from my silver mirror.
A Cornish Lorelei!

People heard
and ran to Bude.

From Stratton, Kilkhampton,
Welcombe and Stowe,
from Coombe and Trebarrow
and hamlets round,
people gathered on the Mound.
They shot torch-lights
down on me. They saw
all they wished to see.

5

Hardy Holcombe
espied
at half-tide
despite the blur
of a slight fog,
"the bootifullest merry-maid."

I twisted my sea-weed hair
to enhance my concealment there
and pretended I was Hardy's sweetheart.

When he seized my straggly locks
I dove from the rocks,
topsy-turvy.

## 6

Bill Gryde
reported "music in the sea"
and a "merry-maid very plain" swimming.
The voice (and here he roared)
evoked *The Reverend Vicar's*
singing second counter in the Service.
Gryde saw breasts—damn my corpulence!
and was amazed by a pizzle,
and an absence of scaly nether parts.

If he guessed the truth
Old Bill confessed it to no one.

## 7

When I'm bedecked and nude,
I am part human, part finny creature,
a presence in the deep
where so many sailors sleep
snuggled in the eiderdowns
of Eternity's hot-gilt
rainbow-tinted bedroom.

# PART FOUR:
## POOR DROWNED SAILORS

# ON CORNISH WRECKERS AND WRECKING

Tell
how earlier clerics
condoned *wrecking*, that dismal
luring of ships
by placing false beacon-lights.

Cognac and amontillado
were thrown up on shore,
with tide-streams
of drowned sailors.

Tell
of stowing kegs in the church
to hide them from the King's men.

Tell
how the parson preached
against drink, knowing
of the King's cutter
rounding the bend, in chase.
At the parson's sign
the wreckers rolled kegs
to caves above the sea.

Tell
how I have terminated all thievery.
Wreckers are anathema to me,
as are Dissenters.
In my pulpit
I hold God's lantern high,
as a guide to salvation.

# TWO FORMER WRECKERS

## 1

Peter Barrow
of desultory but harmless life,
forty years a wrecker,
had no peer in discovering
flotsam and jetsam.
Together we dragged drowned men
up the gorge (450′)
and buried them.

## 2

Tristam Pentire
was a light, wiry
half-stooped man, bent
as if he had a brace of kegs
upon his shoulders.
Sixty-five years of cunning,
and a nose with a red blaze
from that fierce fiend alcohol.

He was my servant of all-work.
He rollicked through his life,
a wondrous lazy man.
I miss his gander.
When I pass his grave
I drop violets
and a robin's egg.

He was the last Cornish smuggler.

# SMUGGLER HORSES

The small shaved horses
of smugglers
smoother than any modern
clips
well-greased from head to
foot,
slip easily from any grasp.

Kegs and packs
of artifacts
secured by a single
girth.

This herd
led
by a driverless mare
fetch the loot
to a cave
and wait there
for the owners
to disburden and de-grease them.

They can not well-strengthen their masts.
They can not spread their sail.
The prey of a great spoil is divided.
The lame take the prey.
Thy tacklings are loosed, O Lord.


I write the following verses on a rock by the shore
where we retrieved six lost sailors.  It (my poem)
may sound quaint, I know, but do, please, hear me out:


63

# THE STORM

War! Mid the ocean and the land!
The battle-field Morwenna's strand,
Where rock and ridge the bulwark keep,
The giant warders of the deep!

They come! and shall they not prevail,
The seething surge, the gathering gale?
They fling their wild flag to the breeze,
The banner of a thousand seas!

They come, they mount, they charge in vain,
Thus far, incalculable main!
No more! thine hosts have not o'erthrown
The lichen on the barrier stone!

Have the rocks faith, that thus they stand
Unmoved, a grim and stately band,
And look, like warriors tried and brave,
Stern, silent, reckless, o'er the wave?

Have the proud billows thought and life
To feel the glory of the strife,
And trust one day, in battle bold,
To win the foeman's haughty hold?

Mark, where they writhe with pride and shame,
Fierce valour, and the zeal of fame;
Hear how their din of madness raves,
The baffled army of the waves!

Thy way, O God! is in the sea;
Thy paths where awful waters be:
Thy Spirit thrills the conscious stone;
O Lord! Thy footsteps are not known.

(c. 1870)

# OFF BUDE, CORNWALL (21 October 1862)

A hull wallowing in the billows.
She struck sand close to the breakwater.
Stout and sinewy forms surround me,
wielding iron bars, pickaxes, ropes.
We fire a rocket over the ship.
The Mate tumbles into the sea, drowned.
Our life-boat refuses to put off,
fearing the waters.  Wesleyan Sneakism, I say!
Shriekings.  All Bude line the cliffs
and shore.  Thirty-five fellows launch
a hasty raft, which is soon tossed over.
Four corpses.  Six men with life in them.
Twenty-six washed out to sea.
The County pays five shillings per corpse.
I pay five more.  The inquests nearly
kill me.

# ON TRYING TO REACH A SHIP IN DISTRESS

### 1

The tide
drives us baffled from the spot
before we can grasp or shake
the ship's mass.

Rifted stone rises and hurls
along the shuddering marge.
The ship lies in smithereens.

### 2

Bloated bodies ride
in the shallows:
a mate and three men.
None has the placid mien
of those drowned by accident,
or of those dead in their beds.
An officer's countenance is grim.
Was he driven from his deck
by a crew despising him?

## 3

Most sailors
have pricked their arms with tracery—
initials, wreaths, anchors, and
forget-me-nots.
I record these marks in the church-log.
These poor dear men assumed
that such pictures would illume
their identities.

What resignation!
to wear on your living flesh,
as if it were for forever,
your sepulchral name.


*Churchwarden:* "Why, Sir, when we used to find dead sailors on the shore, and carried them in, you didn't so give way, as you do now, weeping when you go into the Church."

*Hawker:* "Spare me the misery and, indeed, the proximity, to those far advanced in decay! A debasing terror. A dying sailor. A driven leaf frightens me helter-skelter. Tick-tick. Death-day. Mine."

# THE WRECK OF THE CALEDONIA *(September 1842)*

I rush out
in dressing-gown and slippers.
The lad is trembling,
holding out to me
a live tortoise.
He found it on the sand,
a marvel of a creature
from the waves, knelling
a wreck.

We hurry.  On a ridge
left bare by the tide
is a servant.
He was tending ewes
when he spied the wreck.
Two dead sailors lie at his feet.

Rocks and water bristle
with broken mast, spar, and timber.
The rollers tumble in
corn, the wheaten cargo.
Bodies of the helpless turn
disfigured faces to the sky,
pleading for sepulture.

Ever and anon, I spy
a human hand or an arm.
A corpse drifts out to sea.
One sailor opens his eyes—
Edward de Dain, of Jersey.

Sadly we fetch the sailors
up the cliff, by a difficult path,
to the church.
We array the corpses
on biers of broken planks.

On the captain's grave
we erect the figurehead of a ship,
a carved image, life-sized
of his native Caledonia,
with sword and shield.
I compose these verses:

> We laid them in their lowly rest,
>    The strangers of a distant shore;
> We smoothed the green turf on their breast,
>    'Mid baffled Ocean's angry roar;
> And there, the relique of the storm,
> We fixed fair Scotland's figured form.

> She watches by her bold, her brave,
>    Her shield towards the fatal sea:
> Their cherished lady of the wave
>    Is guardian of their memory.
> Stern is her look, but calm, for there
> No gale can rend or billow bear.

> Stand, silent image! stately stand,
>    Where sighs shall breathe and tears be shed,
> And many a heart of Cornish land,
>    Will soften for the stranger dead.
> They came in paths of storm; they found
>    This quiet home in Christian ground.

# PART FIVE:
# WITCHES, WARLOCKS,
# AND CHARACTERS

Beating rain, howling wind
through chimneys.

Ghosts, pale eyes
soundless—but the words, *felt*,
thrill, as echoes.

# BEWITCHED ANIMALS

At Rokeby a sow
rejects her piglets.
They pine, squeal, and sit upright
on their hinder parts,
touch their paws in piteous fashion,
and, one by one, they die.

Cows go mad.  Those milky mothers
rush from field to field,
their tails the erect poles
of distressed ships
scudding in a gale.

All this Cherry Parnell hath done, they say.
Sprinkle her with witch milk.
Fetch faggots.
Bring her to me.

# WEBBY PRYCE

"Yes," I promise the vestrymen,
"I will examine her.
If I note five black marks on her palate
you may flog her from the hamlet."

Webby lives in a hovel on the down,
sleeps with goats (so gossip owns).
She had a sailor boy, a fair lad
who was lost off the Lizard.
He sleeps now in my churchyard.

"Webby," I say, "this won't take long."
I glance past her black tooth prongs.
Three snags, not Satan's five!
"She is no witch!" I exclaim.    "She is shriven!"

# BLACK JOHN

How strange you are,
you humped, elfin-haired provocateur
of mice and sparrows.

    The lilac blossom
    and the thistle, master,
    burnish the rose.

In your loose, black, flabby mouth
your teeth have long since ceased
to harmonize.

    Go faster sparrow,
    or he'll nab you.
    Scurry, mouseling
    To your wainscot corner.

How many shillings did you earn
for "mumbling" birds, deformed black
jester, or for swallowing mice?
You slept curled, in all weather,
under hedgerows.

    Tie a sparrow to a string
    attached to a tooth.
    "Mumble" off all feathers
    by mouth alone, including
    those encircling the fundament,
    until the bird shivers, bare.
    Secure a mouse-leg by a cord,
    then swallow the creature.

Its toes scratch your throat.
Its fur induces coughing.
When we shout for the mouse,
it yanks forth, saliva-drenched
and puling.

    Rose-water flicked
    by your vicar, John.
    Engorge angels, not shrews!
    Twitter hymns sweeter
    than any sparrow's song!

You spew rage.
I mean your good, Black John.

# TONY CLEVERDON, ANIMAL HEALER

"O, Tony Cleverdon," says he,
"Farmer Colly's mare is bleeding.
Pray do come and save her."

"I won't," says Tony, "for I'm a-bed,
with a wooly night-cap on my head.
Just say the mare's name instead."

"Come! Thou must! A-lack, a-lay.
She won't last another day.
She hath no name. We call her 'Black,'
and that's the gist, no more to say."

"True names you must award your cattle,
or my charms won't work, despite your prattle.
I can hear your mare's death-rattle."

He would have intoned *Ezekiel* twice:
"When thou wast in blood, be alive" —
spliced with an outblow of his breath
and the prick of his thumb,
with a thorn from Christ's crown.

*Out with Evil! Out with thorn!*
*Rub the mare with a greased ram's horn!*
*Happy are we that Christ was born!*

# CHRISTIANA MANNING

Christiana Manning
floats towards me in her bedding,
her frilly lace asunder.
Nor is it any wonder,
for her wraith is mad.

In 1546 she died
when servants fetched her John inside
all gored and torn
by a red bull's horn.

Christiana saw the bloody corpse,
shrieked and started to abort
the five-month foetus in her womb.
She joined her husband in the tomb.

As a wraith she visited me
when I bought a bedstead in '43.
Above some ancient inlaid veneer
was her name, and John's name, clear.
Their espousal bed.

She weeps and moans,
wipes bloody fingers over the bones
of her name, shivers and disappears,
leaving a ringing in my ears.

My old wife whiffles in her sleep.
I draw up her night-shift and insert it deep.
"Christiana," I murmur, "my lost delight,
with your rosy breasts and your ivory thighs so tight."

# FIRST STORM IN PARADISE

It stormed in Paradise:
the primordial fruits athirst,
a water-rat alarmed
by the drying-up
of his stream-bed.
Eve recumbent
on a couch of wet, soaked roses?
She must have prayed for rain
without ever having seen any.
Termites and the insect tribes
wiped their mandibles
and cracked seeds,
edible meats
choked with moisture.
The fowl, in flocks, swooped down.

Water surged through Paradise.
Twigs splashed showers
over our first parents' faces.
Nature gave no shelter.

Eve chid Adam
for not knowing where to hide.
Eve found a cave
and went inside.
Adam meekly followed.

They breathed polluted air
fouled by dust
stirred up by bats, by lizards
with horny plates,
ghastly tongues,
and the wild eyes of basilisks.

# HOW TO GAIN THE EVIL EYE

Go to the chancel, go to sacrament.
Hide there.  Steal meat
from the vicar's table.
Carry the feast (God's body)
all round the church,
widdershins, from south to north,
thrice crossing by east
to the Devil's Porch.
You'll meet a venomous toad
with jaws agape.  Insert
the loaf.  Wait.
He'll regurgitate on your face.
You're a warlock forever.

## ALL IS THE IDEA, THE IDEA IS ALL

I remain sceptical
of a man's reasoning—
whether he arrive
on mule-back or in a phaeton,
dressed as a potato,
an electricity kite,
a Methodist, or a potentate.

We meet on a plateau
of perfect tedium:
*Come in.*
Your ideals or mine?
White sunshine
or orange moonshine?
Do you find a gaol
bewildering or gorgeous?
Is a prig better than a pig?
A tapir better than a pepper-corn?
Did the Sphinx cut her own throat?
Who hung upside down
in the Garden of Babylon?
Are you a Ranting Methodist?
Staunch your Latitudinarianism
as you would a cow's haemorrhage,
with a pink lamb-skin.

Vesuvian laughter:
broad-mouthed, gap-toothed, cataractical.
A lover wrestled with Providence
dropped his pants
and jiggled pasty hams.

Are you not dulcified? transmogrified?
Why are you here?
Expecting beer?
It's dinner-time.
Nibble on this savory chine, of roast-swine.

Oh, here comes Mr. Alfred Tennyson
to sniff my poems and eat my venison.
Belch and depart? No other retort?
An excellent resolve, Sir.
Leave now. Show an elliptical gait.
Here's your hat.

We remain in tedium,
afloat in Babylon.

## PASTORAL ADVICE

I am a man of Byzantine notions.
Do you limp, friend?
A wet toad slumbers
on your chin-wart.
And, you, aren't you the possessor
of the two-legged dog
and the one-spurred Cochin China cock?
Mary Please, why do you sneeze
so often during my sermons?
Clearly, your bourdon-sounds are clearly
supernatural.
Dame, so long as your face
drains juice from its sink-hole ulcer
thou shalt not die.

# MEMENTO MORI RAGOUT

A veiled skeleton
sits in state, at a massive table,
lifting a cypress wreath
above its head.

Skeletal guests
raise flagons of blood
and clap their jaws—
the effect
more cachinnatory
than eerie.

Stewards serve
a Yule ragout
of stewed toads and vipers
spiced with gallstones
sliced warts and boils.
A scorpion fricassee follows.
For dessert, apples of Sodom
and juicy ferret eyes
dipped in chocolate
sweetened with rum.

From the densest gloom
a radiance flashes, crystal,
bright as star-flame,
glowing over those mysteries
driving us insane.

# PART SIX: *OPIUM*

# ON TOOTHACHES AND OPIUM

With toothpain
searing my jaw,
great maxillary fire,
scorched thumb-end,
I scream for anodynes,
yelling hot syllables
unabashed
to the crashing surf
startling my lambs
polluting the runnels
and freshets
with the stench
adhering to my tongue,
a pyotic acid-glue.

I keep my galoshes on,
and my yellow poncho,
giving, I am sure,
to passing folk
a semblance of
who I am.
I press poultices of sheepdung
to my face.  A horny-bee stings me.

The young flee my stench.
Even babes, as they are baptized,
squeal and squirm.
Shall I ever kiss my old wife again?

## 2

Trespass against trespass,
my father suffered for years
until he had his teeth extruded,
except for a pair of molars
eaten too far below the gum-line
to be hooked by the apothecary's
instrument. Like sand, the edges
crumbled, or, like chalk.
My sire's pestilence afflicted
the room he sat in.

## 3

". . .hardly a household in Europe" is free of
toothache, "each in turn having some one chamber
intermittingly echoing the groans extorted by this
cruel torture." —Thomas De Quincey, *Confessions of an
Opium-Eater*.

## 4

I chanced upon a tinker
at an out-door fair.
He was all in motley
with whale-bone in his hair.

I was seated on a stile
in the worst of my toothy pain.
I was ready to rise, shake off my sloth,
and start for my home again.

"It's my ache," I muttered sadly.
"I can hardly see."
"Well, my friend," he said,
"I have something good for thee."

He took from out his waistcoat
a sack of purple hue.
"This will cost a twopence.
You'll be ecstatic when you're through."

He lit a pipe with powder white
and bad me take a draw.
"Your tooth is but a lily now,
as cool and pure as straw."

And he was right! He'd struck a nerve
with anodyne so sweet,
I was so free I danced about
with silver slippers on my feet.

"It's of the exotic poppy.
And I can sell you more.
You won't find any better stuff
along the Cornish shore."

I raced home in a blissful state,
freed at last of pain.
The sky was filled with laughing eyes.
Angels danced in the rain.

# OPIUM

A tawny panacea
bought for a penny.
Peace of mind corked
in a pint-bottle, sent down
by mail-coach.

Laudanum is a tincture
of opium and wine.
Opium never intoxicates,
as wine does.
The pleasure of wine
mounts to a crisis,
then declines. Opium
persists for hours,
a flickering transposing
to a glow,
inducing
a most ardorous harmony.

I am the Pope (consequently
infallible) of the true
Church of Opium, the self-
appointed *legate a latere*
to all degrees
of latitude and longitude.

# TURKS AND ENGLISHMEN

Turks and opium eaters
absurdly sit
like equestrian statues
on logs of wood.
Not so the Englishman
with his laudanum negus,
warm, without sugar.
He rushes to hear Grassini sing.
He scribbles poems, epiphanies.
He encounters knotty alleys
enigmatical entries, dead-ends
without soundings.
He isolates himself
before open windows
for the duration
of the drug's fermentation.
He's in a sabbath of repose,
his brain composed,
a halcyon calm.
O just and subtle, O mighty opium!

# FISTULAS

Tell them
that king Rastafori appeared to me
By adding a boy
to my concubines, he said,
the great fistula on my rump
would burst and heal.

Tell them,
King Rastafori said,
that he was liming pigeons
when he found a sweet goatboy.
The King was in his litter,
in much pain,
in a triumphal procession.
"Stop!" He raised a jewelled finger.
"Bring that lad to me."

I find a boy at St. Ives—
indigo-colored, with
carmine lips and orange gums.
His knee caps are blue.
His buttocks salmon-hued.

*Peters*, I tell you,
I have need of lamb today,
nicely roasted, and of a silver veil
to drape round my buttocks.
Later I shall kiss the boy's
plum-colored lips
and force him against my backside.
Once through, I shall say prayers,
give him a shilling,
and send him home.

## OPIUM PIPE

Ivory maggots
squirm from ivory eyes
in a most ingenious interlacing,
through, round and about.
The skull once held a lady's orbs,
like autumn skies
sweet for dreaming.

## FALSE TEETH

Dentists (none does otherwise)
extract false teeth from corpses.
The Holsworthy dentist is also a farrier.

My teeth have all rotted away.
My mouth is noxious from tooth decay.

All corpse-teeth rot
*sympathetically*
in a stranger's mouth.
Molars are riper than cuspids or incisors.

Clap a dead man's teeth in your jaws
and you'll exude a cloud so foul
you'll be known henceforth as *Carrion*.

I'll never wear a corpse's teeth,
no matter how bright and pearly. Verily
my ministry shall be toothless.

# THE TENTACULA OF CANCER

I cannot face misery.
I am too much the eudaemonist.
I miss my wife Charlotte greatly.
Grief wells in my digits
and through my body.
My heart is stone.
The tendrils rushing my blood hither
scald. Below, cancer-flowers
burgeon in my viscera.
Their stamens and pistils
shiver with pain, assemble
as gaseous pressure
resulting in diarrhea
(I have had to quit my pulpit
more than once of late,
during sermons).

I increase my opium take
to a thousand drops per day.
The gloomy umbrage of my mind
dissolves. Tentaculae of cancer
wither away.

My mouth is packed with ocean sand.
    Farewell to couch and pillow.
My navel and my ears are crammed
    With fishy jellies from the billow.

No longer shall I see my flock—
    Wassailers cease their revels—
Nor clasp my sweet old Charlotte's smock,
    Nor jig and swill with the devil.

The grouse fly up.  The fox are nigh.
    The owl hoots o'er the river.
But I don't see them, as here I lie,
    With sharks shredding my liver.

# FLAME TONGUES

A fire-eyed defiance,
a primrose in flames,
a violet dancing
on a burning kindling-stick.
Counsel of the night,
with your flickering forked tongue,
go hence!
Damn your slavering throat!
You may not *have* me
though you have me.
I am drenched in my own urine,
a scum, a pyogenic vicar
puling and whining
in a cat's cradle of bacon strips
and rennet tissue.

Porphyry, opal, emerald, and chrysolite:
A water-rat's tongue.
Bream-eyes strung
on silver filaments.
A cock's green throat
riddled with maggots.
A lady's white muslin coat
and embroidered slippers.
A ravenous crayfish
with cancerous nippers.
A porcine beadle
anxious to do me hurt.
Porphyry, opal, emerald, and chrysolite.

I'll put my enemies to flight!
I'll burn their jewelled palaces tonight!

Porphyry, opal, emerald, and chrysolite.

# PRISON HALLUCINATION

Evening clangs.
I stuff a keyhole with paper.
I am bolted in.

Six paces north
I meet him
bathed in candle-flame.

He shuffles outside the door.
Iron bolts are no impediment.
Who, pray, is the shadow?
Is he the wind?

He stirs the ashes.
A face seen
in a round brass andiron screen.
The face is mine!

In gleaming snow, in moonlight,
my church tower is a minaret.
Owls with eyes ablaze
turn round
and without a sound
ravish the stray mice
of the populace.

Snowy perfume kiss
the jewelled fields.
Near a whortleberry
I fill my hands with ice . . . .
Salome's red navel
ablaze with rubies!

Pasha, grind my teeth with stones!
Gorge my nostrils with hot tar!
On such a night as this
the Magi saw the Holy Star.

# OPIUM HAZE CHRISTMAS POEM

My terrified wife
is by my bed.
Her hands drip wax.
Her eye-holes are bleached purple,
a noumenal shade.
I drift, to the clang
of cutlery banging on metal,
to the clack of teeth
in an iron kettle.

Brawny legs in violet gaiters
float near the ceiling.
A drowned sailor's breast.
Skeletal hands grasp for others
lurking in a beam.
A stubbled tongue protrudes
from a swirl of ivy
in a glass.

I hear everything:
the cat's saliva drool,
the furry spider on my cheek,
the plop of an egg from a hen,
a sand-sift of voices mellifluous,
like pulled-taffy
in the hands of my mother
at Yuletide.

In sun-stroke
my children
crowd round my bed.
I see their Christmas shoes,
their worsted stockings,
their frocks, their gay hair ribbons.

I take each satiny child-face
and kiss and kiss
until my dear wife draws
the darlings from me
fearing I will bruise them.
I am so drugged!

## OPIUM SONG

The moon is lightless
and my wrist is soft as is my ankle.
A hedgehog scurries.
He sees, in the interstices,
a morsel of great interest.
        Yes, and what do I see?
Blurs on a hedge, a piney sweep,
my old wife's unwashed hair
spread over a rope to air.
        No insects chirr.
The arching sky.  I shall strip
and permit love
its undulations above
the shimmering gorse.
        I see the sea
in a hairy chestnut tree.

I sing this over and over again.
I sing it in throaty octaves
and shall walk no further this year.

# A LAST WORD

*Peters*, I watched as you ran through that storm, over my glebe-lands, to the cliffs where my Hut still stands, the smallest National Trust Property in the British Nation.

I saw your friends Janine Dakyns (to whom I owe gratitude for acquainting you with my story) and Paul Trachtenberg huddled against a stone wall to keep from being drenched by that cold, sleety rain. I appreciate your testimony, and should like to support you, from my vantage-point here in Eternity.

Why, though, did it take you so long to remember my name? H A W K E R ! I shouted it at you over the moors. At the manor house, in Devon, with the Dakyns, you even copied my name out, to memorize it, and you failed.

Only when I stood by your bed, in California, at 3 A.M., in November, and nudged you, and recited that fistula poem, and that one-liner, and told you how to generate the poem you now employ as a frontispiece, could you easily recall my name. I expected better of you. Were you afraid of me?

To present matters: You've been accurate about my various selves: vicar, mermaid, antiquarian, visionary, animal-lover, rescuer of dead sailors, opium taker, father. But I should not have been so needlessly gross in my own poems as you have in yours. Also, when you see me enamored of a milkmaid with cow-pox . . . . Given to such isolation as I knew in those remote Cornish reaches, I did upon occasion chance upon some one of the fairer sex, a damsel of the earth, who did not find my advances unseemly.

I am most grateful for your writing about my black pig Gyp. But you should have written also of my poor dear pony Carrow. I loved him equally. He deserves an acrostic poem of his own. As for the Gyp piece, I'd smooth it a bit, about ¾ths of the way through. You cheat on the style there, on the cadences.

I like several of the poems you have *invented* from Nathaniel Hawthorne. I admired this writer. Not much else in America interested me. And I am glad to see touches taken from De Quincey; he would have understood me better than you have.

Here's a sore point: you imply that my obsession with retrieving dead sailors and burying them in my Churchyard, and my fondness for playing mermaid, reflect a latent homosexuality—in my time we called it *Uranianism*. Be assured that I loved sailors, and hired several of them as my servants. And I seldom went about my clerical duties without wearing some article of sailor dress—sweater, boots, slicker. But what's amiss? Both men and women are God's creatures (male and female created he them). We should love each sex equally. I still despise parsons who hunt and shoot, as I do the gentry who hunt and shoot!

*Peters*, my preference was always for women. And, remember, the sailors I retrieved were often already green with maggoty decay, a state hardly calculated to include erotic thoughts, even in the most jaded psyches. Methinks, *Peters*, you may be trying too hard to see yourself in me. I warn you (in a friendly way, of course) against that.

My first, most encompassing, love was for my church, for the Holy Saint Morwenna, and from my parishioners. Even in my later opium-drenched years, I neglected neither Saint nor Believer. The godly Morwenna was the constant companion of my physical decline. She approved of my death-bed conversion to Roman Catholicism—I know she did. As for my flock, their privations hurt me deeply. You reflect well my behavior towards them.

108

As for opium. I smoked it occasionally, but drank it as a powder mixed with wine, as laudanum, in the customary way. You err, badly, *Peters*, in ascribing to me the ownership of that repellent pipe, the one you imagine of jade or ivory, carved with the image of an erotic maiden in an advanced stage of maggots and death. There were memento mori enough in my life, *Peters*, without having to possess such an artifact. But, then, poets are liars. Why should you be an exception?

I was a poet, too, you know, and a damned good one, admired by Lord Tennyson himself, who paid a call on me. Speaking of my verses, I do appreciate your *deigning* to incorporate a few stanzas of my own, if helter-skelter, throughout your book. You have been niggardly though, and I must complain. Were you fearsome that more poems by me might detract readers from yours? Who is, finally, *Peters*, the better poet?

I should like to see my "The Quest of the Sangraal" reprinted, with a preface by you. Also, my Cornish national anthem must never be forgotten:
And shall Trelawny die?
Here's twenty thousand Cornish men
Will know the reason why!

Finally, *Peters*, I hope that on your next visit to Cornwall, you will visit Morwenstowe again, on a sunny day, and spend a few hours sitting in my hut gazing down that awful precipice (450') at the sea crashing where all those ships foundered. I promise to visit you. Perhaps we can share that pipe? You bring the opium. I've missed it dreadfully.

Yr. obed. servant,

Robert Stephen Hawker

PHOTO BY MAX YEH

Robert Peters lives in Southern California where he teaches Victorian literature and writing workshops in an MFA program. He has published some twenty volumes of poetry since 1967, volumes which reflect a considerable range of form and theme. His earliest books (including *Songs for a Son* and *Cool Zebras of Light*) are intensely personal. A generous representation from these books appears in his *Gauguin's Chair: Selected Poems*. His latest book *What Dillinger Meant to Me* returns to the personal mode, and treats his boyhood in northern Wisconsin on a sub-culture poverty-stricken farm. *The Gift to Be Simple: A Garland for Ann Lee*, is in another of his modes, the persona book, to which *Hawker* belongs. His *The Picnic in the Snow: Ludwig II of Bavaria* is an ambitious treatment of the life of the mad Bavarian king, employing a variety of closed and open forms. For nearly two years he has been acting in his own one-man stage version of the work. He has taken the play to various colleges and universities, including Yale, Brown, Queens, Radcliffe, the Universities of California at Irvine and Riverside, Wisconsin, and Beloit College. He recently completed other voice books: one is by a man obsessed with Robert Mitchum, another by the Hungarian Blood Countess, Elizabeth Bathory, who believed she could perpetuate her youth by bathing in the blood of virgins. She was immured in her castle, in 1611, after decimating some 700 women. Unicorn Press will also publish his *Elisha Kent Kane*, an excursion into the mind and voice of the famous American Arctic explorer. He next projects a treatment of the tragic British painter Benjamin Robert Haydon.

Peters is also widely known as an iconoclastic critic. His two *Great American Poetry Bake-off* volumes have been praised by Robert Bly and other critics as among the most original works of American criticism in recent years. His *Peters Black and Blue Guide to Literary Periodicals* is currently stirring up much controversy. He is contributing editor for the *The American Book Review*, and *Contact II*. He is also editing an ambitious series of Selected American Poets, "Poets Now," for Scarecrow Press. Six of these are already published. Peters is a skilled parodist, and has contributed to the *Brand-X Anthologies* of Poetry and Fiction. His *The Poet as Ice-Skater* contains several of his parodies of other poets, living and dead.

Finally, Peters is an idefatigable jogger, and receives many of his ideas for poems and critical pieces while on the move. He lives a serene life, aided and abetted by fellow-poet Paul Trachtenberg. His three children, grown, are at large in the world. His daughter Meredith, who works in the library at the UN, has provided drawings for several of his books. Among his many awards are a Guggenheim Fellowship, a National Endowment for the Arts Grant, and several fellowships to Yaddo, the MacDowell Colony, and the Ossabaw Island Project. *Hawker* was awarded the prestigious Alice Faye di Castagnola Prize, by the Poetry Society of America, in 1982.